Old RUTHERGLEN

by
Rhona Wilson

© Richard Stenlake Publishing 1996
First Published in the United Kingdom, 1996, by Stenlake Publishing
Telephone / fax: 01290 551122
Reprinted 2006
Printed by St Edmundsbury Press Ltd

ISBN 1 872074 72 3

Although the building on the left of this picture of Farme Cross is still standing, the tenement block taking up the bulk of the picture has been demolished and the site landscaped.

This picture of a Rutherglen-bound tram was probably taken at Charing Cross, Glasgow around 1912.

In 1126 King David I granted a charter making Rutherglen a Royal Burgh, which allowed it to develop internal and external trade. Fairs were held regularly, the most important of which was St Luke's. At the time Main Street was one of the broadest in Scotland, its width perfect for accommodating the livestock and traders who came to the town. Rutherglen citizens had the right to sell ale and whisky licence-free to visitors, and fairs were a great excuse for revelry. However, though once important as a place of trade Rutherglen's significance eventually faded, especially in comparison to neighbouring Glasgow whom it once extracted dues from. Ironically, Glasgow was once within Rutherglen's boundaries. The markets ended in 1900.

The Toll House at Rutherglen Cross marked the entrance to fairs held in Main Street, and traders had to pass it and pay dues on the goods they brought into the Burgh. Previously this was the Muirkirk Road, but at the turn of the twentieth century it appears on maps as Stonelaw Road. The red sandstone block of Alexandra Place and the building just visible at the far right hand edge of this picture are still standing, although everything else has now gone. The tall building on the right was one of only two high backed roofs in Rutherglen used for hanging washing on.

THE CROSS, RUTHERGLEN.

Boots Corner at Rutherglen Cross was once a popular meeting place for courting couples. Boots still stands here although the shop has been rebuilt and the flats above it removed. The buildings on the left have been cleared and replaced by various modern ones including Housing Department offices.

STONELAW ROAD, RUTHERGLEN. (9)

222246. J.V.

The vehicle in the middle distance next to the tram was used for checking and repairing the overhead cables for the trams. Further up Stonelaw Road are Stonelaw Woods which were previously part of the Stonelaw Stone Quarry, one of four quarries in Rutherglen. (The other three were Eastfield Quarry, Cathkin Quarry and West Quarry.) Its five acres were opened to the public in 1900 having been saved from development by the Town Council in 1899. The woods are still standing.

STONELAW ROAD, RUTHERGLEN

D 2031

An old Rutherglen meeting place, Marie's Cafe, features in this picture of Stonelaw Road looking north. Much sterner stuff was originally sold on the premises, although the owners of the then Burnside Pub fell foul of the Rutherglen Veto Poll of 1920. With the pub's closure almost the entire south side of Main Street was left dry. The premises were taken over by the Coias, another Italian family, who left the pub fixtures and fittings untouched. The cafe passed to new owners sometime around the 1940s and flourished for another twenty odd years selling nothing more lethal than the ominous enough 'Pink Paraffins'. When it closed in the mid 1960s it was taken over by David Brodie who used it as a car showroom, which gives an idea of its size. The red sandstone block it stood in was demolished in the 1970s during the building of the Arcade.

Rosslyn Terrace in Stonelaw Road, erected by the Rutherglen builder John Love in 1904, was built on the site of one of the old town's major industries, the Stonelaw No.1 Coal Pit. It is not known exactly when the pit opened, but documentation concerning mining there exists from 1595 onwards. Pit owners included, among others, Gabriel Grey (*c.*1770-1788), followed by Major John Spens, owner until about 1821. After remaining in the Reid family for over fifty years the business was taken over by the Farme Coal Company which operated it from 1892 until its closure. The pit head was to the right hand side of the picture, directly behind Rosslyn Terrace, which remains intact today.

There were as many as twenty-five working farms in and around Rutherglen as late as the 1920s, and Stonelaw Farm was situated at the present day corner of Greystone Avenue and Stonelaw Road. From 1841-51 its 110 acres were farmed by William Wallace. Thomas Hamilton was the last farmer (1926-1950), leasing the land from Colonel Buchanan of Eastfield. At that point the farm's size had dropped to thirty-five acres. The farmhouse was demolished by Rutherglen Burgh Council in 1950 to make way for the building of terraced houses on Greystone Avenue. Other farms in the area included Blackfaulds Farm (commonly known as Imries Farm), Crosshill Farm (sometimes known as Bankhead Farm), Spittal Farm and Fishescoates Farm.

Hamilton Road (previously Wardlawhill Street) looking west towards an area once known by locals as the 'drossey brae' due to shale from the coal at Stonelaw Coal Pit. Hamilton Road originally formed the entrance to Gallowflat House, owned by Coal Master Colonel John R. Reid. Archie Yuill, another Ru'glen worthy, is also connected with the street having been born here in 1855. At present, the area remains reasonably intact. The tenement blocks on either side of the picture have been renovated although the two small buildings in the right foreground have been demolished.

Stonelaw Towers stood on Stonelaw Road, and although the history of the building is vague, the tower is thought to have been built in the fifteenth century. At one point it was used to hold winding machinery for the nearby coal mine. One of the early residents was General John Spens, a keen agriculturist credited with beautifying much of the surrounding Stonelaw Estate, who had a hand in planting the Stonelaw Woods. The last resident to live at the Towers was Councillor Alan Tilston, one of the first men to stand for the Scottish Nationalist Party, and instantly recognisable around Rutherglen on account of his kilt. He lived there from the 1930s until the building was vacated in 1963. The Towers was subject to a lot of vandalism and was in a very bad state of repair when its new owners (the Power Petroleum Company) eventually demolished it in 1965. To this day a great part of the enclosure walls remain.

EAST U.F. CHURCH, RUTHERGLEN.

Left: Built in 1872, the East United Free Church is held together from gable to gable by steel bolts (still visible at the rear of the building). It developed structural problems a mere ten years after it opened, reputedly caused by machinery working in Stonelaw Coal Pits Nos.2 and 3, which were just behind it. Owners of the pits bolted the building together in 1884, and compensated the church after legal proceedings in 1896. It re-opened in 1898 and remained in service until the 1980s. At present, the building is boarded up.

Right: The steeple of the old parish church, situated just off Main Street. Blind Harry, minstrel and poet, relayed the betrayal of William Wallace to the English by Sir John Monteith here, and a peace treaty was signed at the church between the Scots and English in 1297. A meeting of Parliament is also thought to have taken place here in May 1300. Local rumours that a secret passage runs from under the tower to Cambuslang are apparently unfounded! A new church was built adjacent to the steeple in 1794, while the present building opened in 1902.

Rutherglen Steeple (12th Century) (12)   80756 J.V.

The origins of this band are unknown. I asked several Ruglonians if they could name it but opinions differed from the Salvation Army (denied by the Rutherglen branch) to Rutherglen Whistle and Flute Band. Maybe a reader will be able to identify them!

This fountain was erected in 1897 to celebrate Queen Victoria's Diamond Jubilee.

By 1911 Queen Victoria was ten years dead, and her son Edward VII was at the end of his days after a mere decade on the throne. The fountain had become an obstacle to the increasingly popular motor car, and was removed to Overtoun Park, where it can still be seen today.

RUTHERGLEN EVANGELISTIC INSTITUTE.

Daniel L. Rodger, who died in 1930, founded the Rutherglen Evangelistic Institute. The Greenbank Street premises were built in 1885 and the Institute, supported financially by Lord Overtoun, celebrated its 50th anniversary in 1935. Saturday night lantern meetings featuring lectures on various topics were an important source of entertainment in Rutherglen especially since they were often followed by a showing of the latest Charlie Chaplin film. During the First World War around 10% of soldiers from Rutherglen gave their religion as the Rodgers' Institute. The building has now been converted into flats.

Mrs D.L. Rodger, who assisted at the Institute, appears in this picture with one of her sons at the family residence, Overtoun House, which still stands in Sherrifpark North Street.

Trams ran in Rutherglen over a sixty year stretch, and this picture shows one of the very early open-top cars near the Burnside terminus. After waiting for rails to arrive from America, the first tram rolled into Main Street to huge crowds on 2nd April 1902. By the end of 1903 Rutherglen Town Council, ever commodious to Glasgow, deigned to allow tram employees the use of toilets at the Town Hall if the Corporation paid for the water used. The Burnside extension, from Main Street along Stonelaw Road, was opened in 1908. Burnside Special School for physically handicapped children opened *c*.1915 and a special track was laid off Stonelaw Road into Grays Avenue to accommodate cars carrying the children into the school.

RHUL PICTURE HOUSE AND BURNSIDE TERMINUS, RUTHERGLEN. (18) 222243.J.V.

The Rhul cinema stood on Stonelaw Road, while the Grand Central, Pavilion (known as 'Greens') and the Odeon (originally the Vogue) were all in Main Street. All of these cinemas have now closed, and the Odeon has been re-invented as the Mecca Bingo Hall.

Burnside Loch, also known as Buttery-burn Loch, was a well known local beauty spot, popular both with Ruglonians and visitors from Glasgow. After improvements were made to it in 1885, the loch was suitable for use as a boating pond in summer as well as a curling and skating rink in winter. It was drained sometime after the end of the First World War.

Bowling is a favourite Ruglonian pastime and there are several clubs in the area. Burnside Bowling Green was established in 1909, some time after the main Rutherglen Bowling Club was founded. Visitors to Rutherglen Museum can see an original Nazi bomb map focusing on Rutherglen's industrial sites. However, disaster struck for Germany in 1941 when a bomber missed the lot and hit the south green at the Rutherglen club instead. Burnside Parish Church stands out of picture to the right. Originally St. Gilbert's Church in Pollokshields, it was rebuilt stone by stone on the present site in the early 1950s.

In 1860, Victoria Gardens' allotment plot was huge, stretching all the way from Farmloan Road, running parallel with the railway line through Castle Street and onto Green Road. The Gardens' Association made their centenary although the site of the allotments was changed a few times; to Alleysbank in February 1880 and Claudesbush, Mill Street in November 1890. This site in Rodger Drive was acquired in 1912 but closed in the 1970s, when the *Reformer* printed articles interviewing outraged members shocked at the Council's proposals to build housing for nurses on the gardens. They vowed to fight all the way to stop building going ahead but were unsuccessful.

Located on the north side of the Cathkin hills, Castlemilk House was actually in the parish of Carmunnock, although most of its estate was in Rutherglen. The exact age of the house is unknown, although at one point it was the family seat of Sir John Stuart, and Mary Queen of Scots is thought to have resided there the night before the Battle of Langside. The room where she slept was named Queen Mary's Room thereafter. The last Laird to stay there was Sir Stirling Stuart, and soon after his death in 1938 the house became a children's home. Castlemilk was later demolished, and house building commenced in the 1970s.

CASTLEMILK. F.C.

In Glasgow at the turn of the century there were hundreds of amateur football teams. On any Sunday at Glasgow Green at least fifty would be playing, and at Ibrox there were fifty pitches with a proportionate number of teams all involved in local Sunday leagues. As a result, information on many of these teams is scant. Castlemilk FC was probably a local team, perhaps made up of some estate workers from Castlemilk Estate.

Glencairn FC photographed during the 1930s.
Back row: W. Whyte (Capt.), R. McNaught, J. Hall, J. McIntyre, W. Sneddon, T. Clark.
Front row: A. Hart, J. Cahill, P. McAteer, J. McGhie, D. Campbell.

The Chookie Hens have a proud history, having won the Scottish Junior Cup four times. They were also Central League Championship winners three times, and produced a number of players who went on to play for Scotland at international level in their later careers. These include Jimmy McMeneny who played for Celtic, Sammy Beard of Rangers and Alex Bennets who played for both Old Firm teams. Bernie Slaven was capped for the Republic of Ireland after a stint at Albion Rovers and Middlesborough. The club have played in their grounds at Southcroft Park for 100 years but will soon be forced to move elsewhere. The M74 motorway extension is taking a route through the park and the Glens will relocate to new grounds on the other side of the railway line.

This part of the Carmunnock Road is within Rutherglen. The cottage was the birth place of the Rutherglen missionary James Gilmour, who was born on the 12 June 1843. He died far from Rutherglen at Tientsin in China on the 21 May 1891.

Calderwood Road runs along the former route of the Whorl Pit Road, once the main route south to East Kilbride . A hundred-yard section of the old road still exists near Langleigh Avenue behind the Cathkin Hotel on the East Kilbride Road. These houses were built around 1905 as the Gallowflat Housing Scheme, and still stand today.

THE OLD ROUND HOUSE, RUTHERGLEN

The Round House stood at the junction of the East Kilbride Road (on the left) and Burnside Road, the main route south to the Cathkin Braes. It is thought that the house got its name from the rounded gable ends clearly visible here. Once a Rutherglen landmark, the cottage was demolished in 1904 to make way for a railway line and eventually became the site of an overhead bridge, station and tramway terminus.

Ruglonian public houses have suffered much over the years. The building in the middle distance with the whitewashed gable end was Johnny Morrison's Burnhill Rest on Chapel Street. It was demolished c.1937 and, confusingly, a new pub with exactly the same name was built diagonally across the street to replace it. In the early 1970s this was wiped out along with five other pubs (including Ye Olde Inn, the Forrester's Arms and the Glencairn Bar) to make way for a dual carriageway heading through Rutherglen to the Cathkin Bypass. The street as seen here has totally changed and is now a busy thoroughfare with various housing schemes on either side.

THE SQUARE, NEW CLINIC AND "RIO" PICTURE HOUSE, RUTHERGLEN   A.9388

By the mid 1930s, Rutherglen had five cinemas. The Rio, at the corner of Glasgow Road and King Street, opened in March 1935. It had a seating capacity of over 2000 (including 30 standing places!) and remained open until around 1970. The first cinema in Rutherglen was the Electric Picture House in Stonelaw Road which opened in 1910. Although it stopped showing films in the 1930s it wasn't demolished until the 1960s and was used as a billiard hall till then. This scene has totally changed now. Both the cinema and the clinic have long gone, to be replaced by housing schemes and the upgraded Mill Street.

SQUARE AND WAR MEMORIAL, RUTHERGLEN. (7)

222242.J.V.

Rutherglen's War Memorial, designed by the sculptor Robert Gray, was unveiled on 26 October 1924.

Mill Street *c.*1908.

COMMERCIAL BANK AND WEST U.F. CHURCH, RUTHERGLEN.

The Commercial Bank building, on the corner of Glasgow Road and Chapel Street, was later used as the offices of the Burgh House Factor. It was demolished in the early 1970s for the same reason as much of old Rutherglen disappeared; to accommodate the new dual carriageway. Built in the mid-nineteenth century, the West United Free Church is still standing, although it became the West Parish Church in October 1965. The white-washed building on the right was known as the 'Back Raw'. This section of the street was obliterated when the war memorial was built.

Mill Street originally led up to the meal mill at Bankhead Estate, hence its name. There are no known photographs of the mill, but a sketch of it appears in Rutherglen Lore and an inscription over the doorway stated that it was built in 1622. The mill closed after Miller Downes was horribly killed after getting caught in the rollers of the grinding machinery about 1865. The last person to reside there was Matthew Jackson, gardener to the last estate owner, Prof. James Quigley. He lived there until 1955 after which the estate was sold with the building eventually being demolished in the early 1970s. The present Mill Street has changed dramatically. It has been developed into a dual carriageway and acts as a feeder for the Glasgow Road. This picture, which looks south along the street, was taken about 1906.

Built in 1905 as one of a block of seven shops, the Overtoun Bakery was on the west side of Mill Street looking up Clincarthill Road. Alex Burlington was the first proprietor and had the shop for around five years. Thereafter it was leased by a Mr Stirling before passing into the hands of the Thompson family where it remained. In the early 1970s a large part of Mill Street was demolished to make way for the dual carriageway and the bakery moved into Wallace Street. The last owner, Alexander Thompson, retired in 1989.

Main Street *c.*1910.

A tram heads towards the Shawfield boundary. The flat above the News Emporium was the birthplace of Ruglonian worthy Dr Gorman and is still standing, as is the large tenement block and the shops on its left. A blacksmith's shop stood on the left of Main Street near where the tram is.

MAIN STREET LOOKING EAST, RUTHERGLEN   A.8452

Rutherglen Co-operative Society – beside the Odeon Cinema – eventually had branches throughout Rutherglen and East Kilbride, plus a fleet of vans which were housed at Chapel Street until around 1963, and Baronald Street thereafter. The head office was at 240 Main Street and the halls were used for local marriage receptions amongst other things. Dividends were the main advantage of the Co-op, and a weekly shop there could earn cash of up to £10 (almost a week's wages at the time) back annually. This building was demolished in the late 1970s and the Co-op is now at the opposite end of Main Street.

MAIN STREET FROM THE CROSS, RUTHERGLEN. 222245.

This picture of Rutherglen in the 1930s shows the extent of the changes in Main Street over the twentieth century. While the north side remains reasonably intact, the tenements on the south side (which replaced low cottages, some of which survived until the turn of the century) have nearly all been replaced by modern buildings. In the late 1940s it was estimated that over 70% of newlyweds in Rutherglen either lived with their parents or went into lodgings. A shortage of housing – which led to overcrowding – meant that epidemics such as tuberculosis were rife since it was impossible to quarantine the ill through lack of space.

Town Hall, Rutherglen.

Rutherglen's extremely grand town hall dominates Main Street, although today it is home to organisations such as the Citizens Advice Bureau instead of bureaucrats. When it opened in 1862 it replaced the Tolbooth as the Town Council's meeting place. In 1876-77, extensions were added to accommodate the police offices, a jail and the new council chamber. Perhaps there was some significance in the council and a bunch of crooks being shacked up together! The main section hasn't been used for civic duties since Rutherglen's status as an independent Royal Burgh ended in 1975, and it has been suggested that it could be converted into flats or used to rehouse Rutherglen Museum. A couple of years ago an exasperated *Reformer* ran a story on April Fool's Day telling tale of an American with Ruglonian blood who was interested in transporting the building to New York. However, no final decision has been made as to its future.

RUTHERGLEN WAR MEMORIAL.

Left: Burnside tram terminus. The arrival of trolleybuses in 1939 heralded the beginning of the end for trams in Rutherglen. Glasgow Corporation authorised a trolleybus extension to Rutherglen Cross in 1955 which took trams off Main Street, although they had a temporary reprieve for a few months in 1956 during the Suez Crisis, replacing some trolleybuses due to fuel shortages. The last tram from Burnside Terminus was the No.18 (now in a tramway museum in Paris) which left, amid crowds, at the beginning of June 1961. For a short time afterwards trams continued to run on the No.26 route from Farme Cross. The service ran for the last time on the 22nd October of the same year.

Right: A 1930s Glasgow Corporation Bus.

Rutherglen Old Arch and Old Residenters. R.B.

The Port Gate, built in 1663, forms the entrance to the parish churchyard. Sentry posts were built within the gates on either side of the entrance, either for protecting elders from rain or to house guards keeping a watch for body snatchers, depending on whom you read! Previously known as St Mary's Churchyard, the area is said to have been a burial ground since the sixth century. There were around 1,450 known lairs in the churchyard, with the first plot belonging to the Gorman family. After 1881, when Rutherglen Cemetery was opened, only lair holders were allowed to use the churchyard for burials and, even then, had to obtain special permission from the local authority. In November 1952 Rutherglen Town Council advertised in the *Reformer* to ask if anyone could still lay claim to burial rights. Only two families replied and the last burial took place around 1953.

Left: Dr Gorman made such an impression on Rutherglen that when he died in 1899 a public subscription was set up to pay for his statue, which stands on the boundary wall of the Old Parish Church. The doctor started work in the district assisting his father, a medical attendant for workmen at the coal pits throughout Rutherglen. He quickly gained a reputation for going to sick people at any time of the day or night and waiving fees for those who couldn't afford them.

Right: The Warnock family has a long history in Rutherglen, and not just as butchers; Hobson and Warnock Builders had a hand in erecting the Town Hall in 1861. Parliamentary Road was the site of the family's first butcher shop. This eventually moved to Main Street in 1929 and kept switching locations from then on. Originally at No 204, as seen here, the shop moved to No 196 and then headed eastwards again when the Arcade was built in 1972. The lamp post outside the Arcade marks where the shop once stood. At the moment there are three branches of the business (the other two are in Wallace Street and Buchanan Drive, Cambuslang) which have been run by the present three Warnock brothers since they left school.

This mill was one of three power loom weaving factories situated within 100 yards of each other in Rutherglen. Initially, the factories could produce only coarse forms of cloth and hand loom weavers were still in demand for intricate work. As the new machinery became more advanced power looms became the norm, although some weavers survived in Rutherglen until as late as 1904. This mill opened sometime before 1851. Although it was called the Burnside Power Loom Weaving Factory it was not located within present day Burnside. Instead, the mill was named after the West Burn (commonly known as Jenny's Burn) on which it was situated. An old local saying conferring prosperity, 'may Ru'glen's roon lums briskly reek', indicates how important industry was to Rutherglen.

This picture, with White's chimneys in the background, recalls another Ruglonian industry. T. B. Seath's ship building business was established in 1856 when he leased two acres on the south bank of the Clyde for use as a launching point. The firm built a variety of different vessels including coastal traders and pleasure steamers such as the *Lucy Ashton* which sailed for 60 years. In all, over 300 ships were built in Rutherglen during its lifetime. The *Isle of Arran* was the last paddle steamer built by the yard, seeing some action when she was converted into a mine sweeper during the First World War. This ship's bell is now used to ring closing time in the Public Library. The diminutive Seath died in 1903 and the business was taken over by another company before closing sometime about 1923.

Farie Street Public School opened in 1875 and closed in 1971 just short of its centenary. The street and school were named after the Faries of Farme Castle, Coal Masters who had a pit in the area at one point. Up until 1923 the school went through only two headmasters, John F Scott and William Guild. The year of the class here is unknown – perhaps readers will be able to work that out. In August 1957 the school became St Colombkilles RC Primary (the cause of much tension in the local community) and was vacated on the opening of a new school in Clincarthill Road in 1969. The old building was eventually demolished and Mill Court Housing Estate built on its site.

Rutherglen Constabulary circa 1923. In 1848 the social activities of Irish navvies working on the Glasgow to London railway line instigated the creation of the Rutherglen Special Constable. Irish workmen were coming up in gangs to Main Street and causing havoc in the pubs, so it was decided to police the general area. Special Constables were assigned a specific beat to patrol and were involved in the 'suppression of riotous and seditious conduct'. Before 1876 the Rutherglen Police Force was based at the Old Tolbooth which had offices and a jail. After this the police station moved to the Town Hall extension which included an upstairs barracks for officers. The cells are now used by the Citizens Advice Bureau as interview booths and the present day police station, built in the mid-1950s, is in King Street.

Regent Street decorated for the King's Coronation visit in 1937. Geordie Mann, former Provost, apparently managed to inveigle his way into the queue of dignitaries lined up to meet the Queen during her visit to Rutherglen in the 1950s. Local folklore has it that when she got to him he pulled out a picture and informed her 'that's me with yer faither in 1937!'

KIRKWOOD STREET, RUTHERGLEN

Although the tenements in Kirkwood Street are still standing, the view at the bottom of the street up Denim's Hill has gone forever. The entire area is built up now, and Rutherglen Swimming Pool (on Greenhill Road) now straddles the bottom of the street.

Overtoun Park bandstand was donated by Sir James Fleming of Woodburn in 1914, and has been put out to work in recent years. When Rutherglen was still within Glasgow District Council's jurisdiction during the late 1980s, the bandstand was loaned to various Garden Festivals around the country. It has since been re-instated about 150 yards to the right of where it is seen here. The park itself, formerly Low Crosshill and Broomieknowe Farms, was bought by James C. White (Lord Overtoun) and donated to the Burgh, opening in May 1908. Lord Overtoun is the only Ruglonian to be honoured with a statue in Glasgow (in Cathedral Square). Overtoun Park, however, is not the only legacy he left behind. A pamphlet published by the Labour Leader and entitled 'White Slaves: Lord Overtoun, Chrome, Charity, Crystals and Cant' gives an alternative account of his influence.

It was estimated by friends of Lord Overtoun that he donated over £10,000 a year to 'causes', and it is worth investigating where he got the cash from. This picture shows White's Chemical Works, in the family since 1810, and at one point the largest of its kind in Europe. By 1840 White's main product was bichromate of potash, originally used for dyes. This product led to a condition known as Chrome Holes, and many plant workers could put a hankie up one nostril and pull it out the other because of cartilage damage from chemical fumes. A report compiled in the early 1990s estimated it would require £20 million to clear up the chromium waste in the Rutherglen area. When the Whites sold out to the Associated Chemical Company in the late 1950s/early 1960s the works were transferred to Stockton-on-Tees. The vehicle in the distance in this June 1955 view is the Planet steam engine used by the works.

CORONATION CHUMS 1937

Coronation Chums 1937, Kirkwood Street residents – do you recognise anyone?